Flowers

Instructions on page 49.

Instructions on page 50.

Instructions on page 51.

3

4

Instructions on page 52.

Instructions on page 53.

5

Instructions on page 54.

Instructions on page 55.

Instructions on page 56.

8

Instructions on page 57.

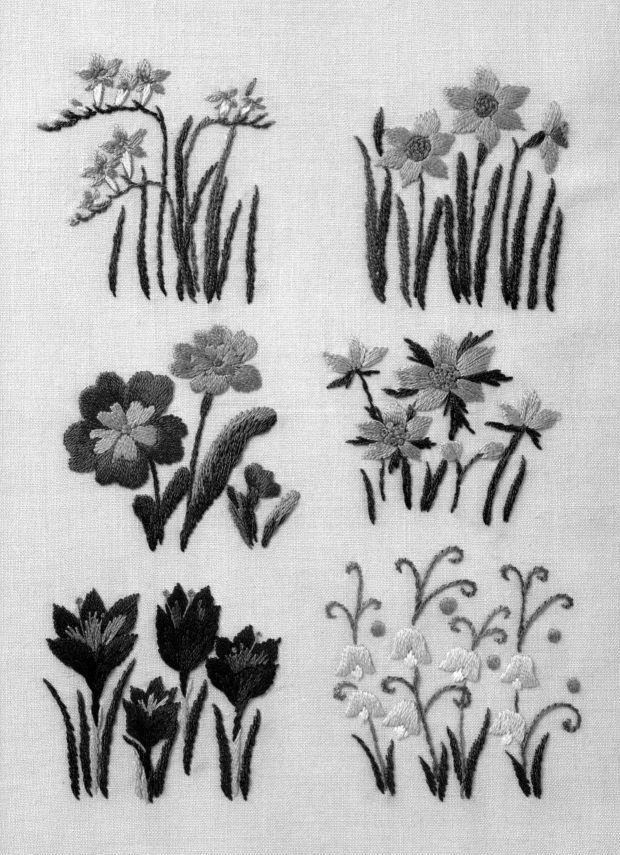

Instructions on page 58.

Instructions on page 59.

11

Good Friends

Instructions on page 60.

Instructions on page 61.

14

Instructions on page 62.

Instructions on page 63.

16

Instructions on page 64.

Instructions on page 65.

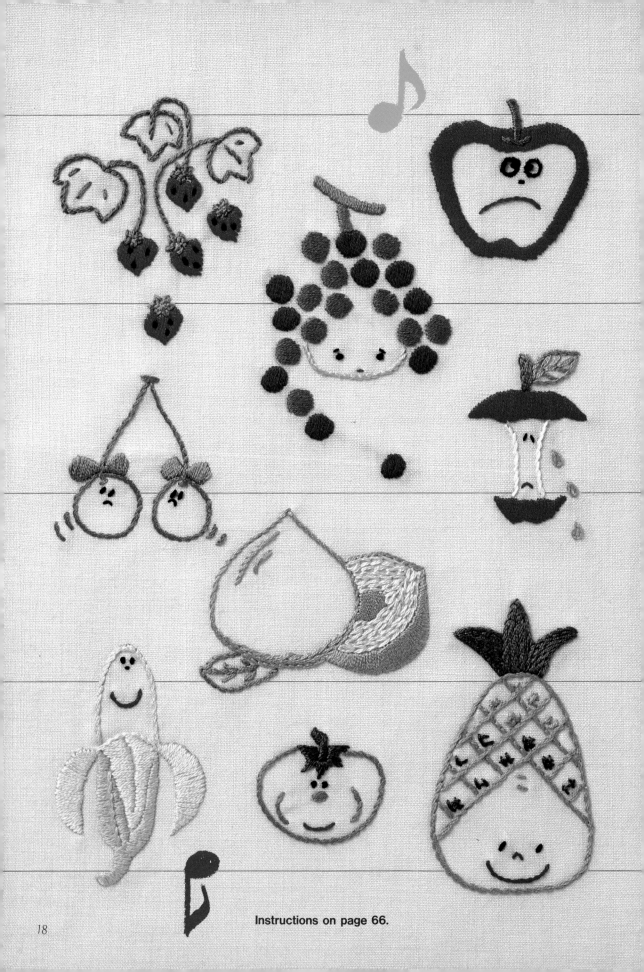

Instructions on page 66.

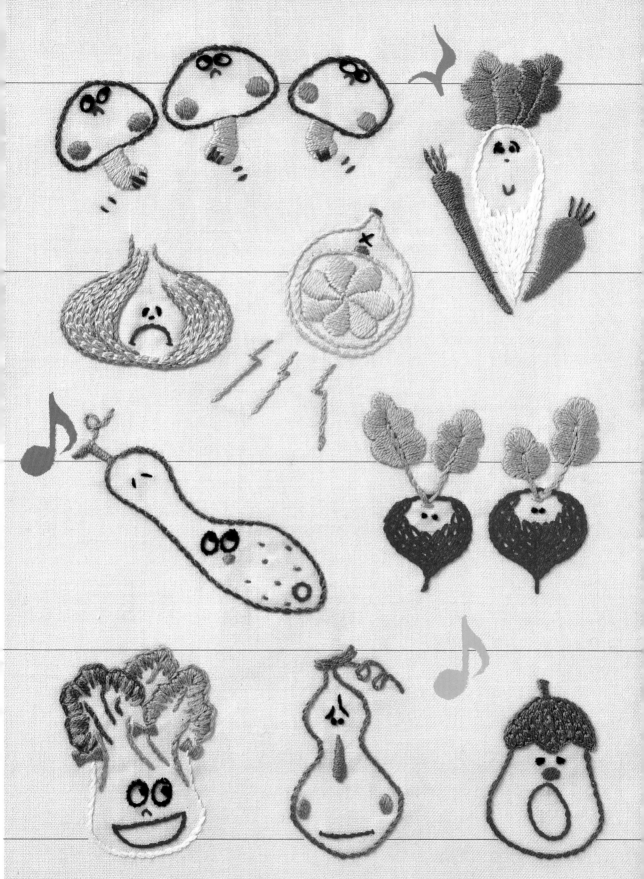

Instructions on page 67.

19

Instructions on page 68.

Instructions on page 69.

Dream

Instructions on page 70.

Instructions on page 71.

24

Instructions on page 72.

Instructions on page 73.

Instructions on page 74.

Instructions on page 75.

Small Accent

Instructions on page 76.

Instructions on page 77.

Instructions on page 78.

Instructions on page 79.

REPEATING PATTERNS

Instructions on page 80.

mush room

carrot . . . . carrot

. . . . Peas . . .

radish   radish

glass

ribbon

cup

box

Instructions on page 81.

Instructions on page 82.

34

Instructions on page 83.

PICTURES

Instructions on page 84.

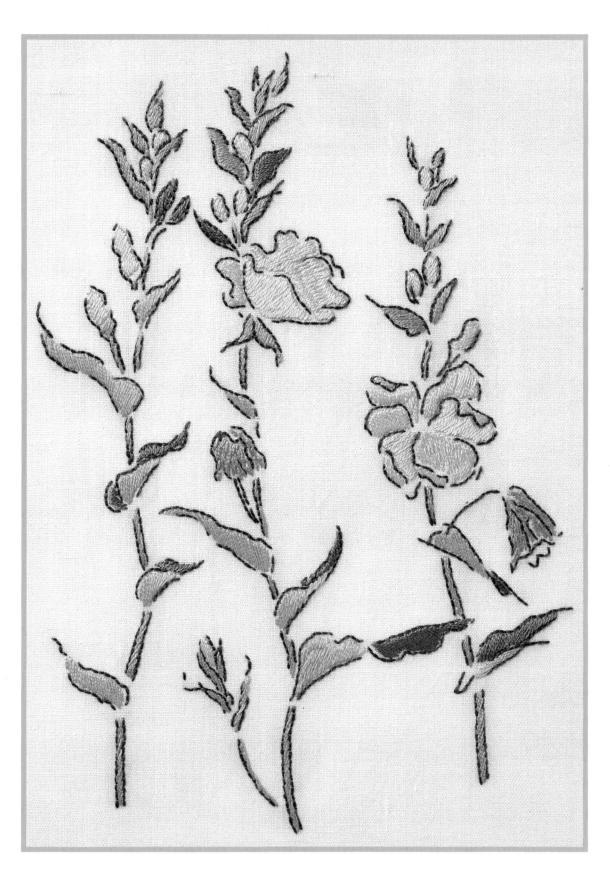

Instructions on page 85.

Instructions on page 86.

Instructions on page 87.

Instructions on page 88.

Instructions on page 89.

ABC ·········· Z

Instructions on page 90.

1 2 3 4 5 6 7 8 9

E F G H
M N O P
U V W

Instructions on page 91.

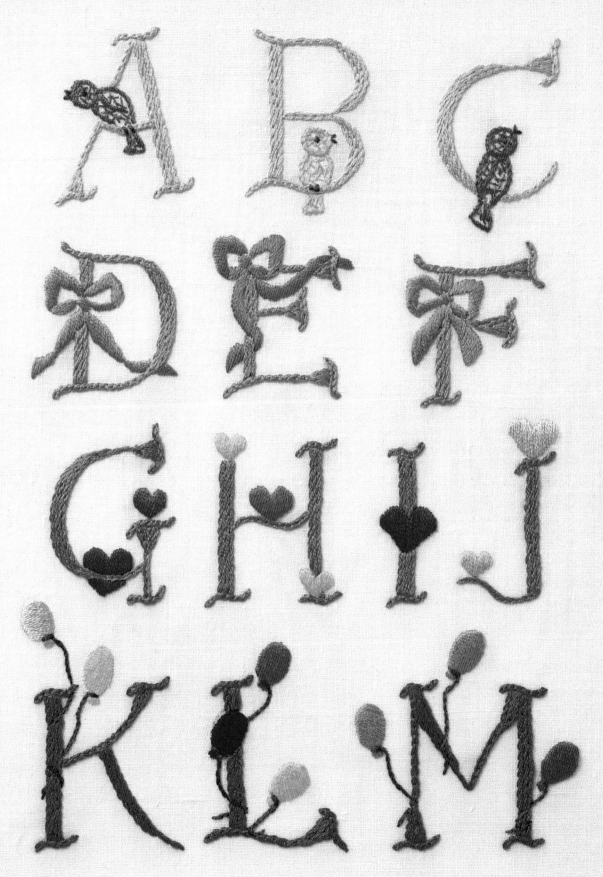

44

Instructions on page 92.

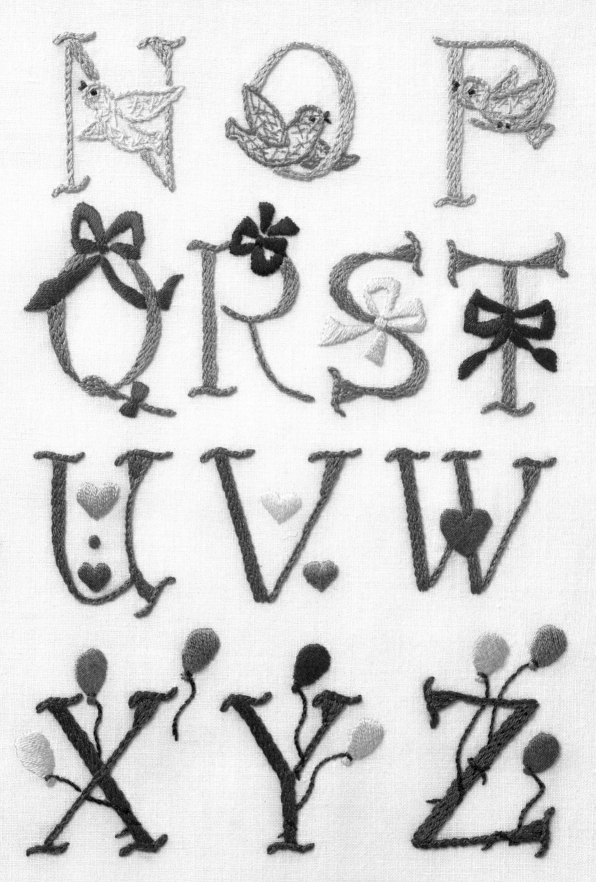

Instructions on page 93.

Gift Tags

Instructions on page 94.

Instructions on page 95.

48

Instructions on page 96.

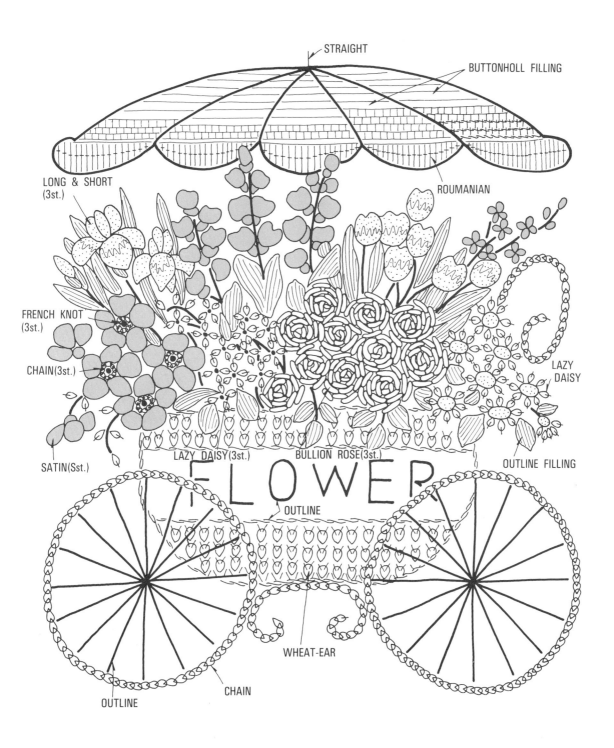

STRAIGHT

BUTTONHOLL FILLING

LONG & SHORT
(3st.)

ROUMANIAN

FRENCH KNOT
(3st.)

CHAIN(3st.)

LAZY
DAISY

SATIN(Sst.)

LAZY DAISY(3st.)

BULLION ROSE(3st.)

OUTLINE FILLING

FLOWER

OUTLINE

WHEAT-EAR

OUTLINE

CHAIN

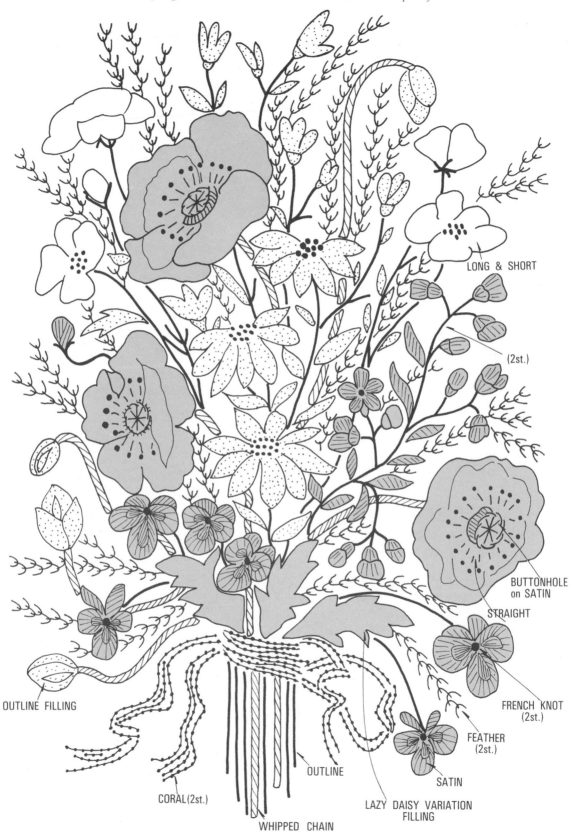

LONG & SHORT

(2st.)

BUTTONHOLE
on SATIN

STRAIGHT

FRENCH KNOT
(2st.)

FEATHER
(2st.)

OUTLINE FILLING

OUTLINE

SATIN

CORAL(2st.)

LAZY DAISY VARIATION
FILLING

WHIPPED CHAIN

NEEDLEWORK on page 3.

3 strands and long & short stirchs, unless otherwise specified.

SATIN

OUTLINE FILLING

FRENCH KNOT

BACK

CHAIN

STRAIGHT(1st.)

FRENCH KNOT FILLING

OUTLINE

CLOSED HERRINGBONE

NEEDLEWORK on page 4. *4 strands, unless otherwise specified.*

CHAIN FILLING

STRAIGHT

OUTLINE FILLING

(2st.)

GERMAN KNOT

SATIN

(2st.)

STRAIGHT(2st.)

CROSS

(2st.)

CORAL FILLING

LONG & SHORT

SURFACE DARNING

CHAIN

OUTLINE

FRENCH KNOT

FLY VARIATION

WHEAT-EAR

CORAL FILLING

OPEN BUTTONHOLE

LAZY DAISY

FLY

NEEDLEWORK on page 5.   *3 strands, unless otherwise specified.*

SURFACE DARNING

LAZY DAISY

OUTLINE

FRENCH KNOT

STRAIGHT (1st.)

BACK(2st.)

(2st.)

TWISTED CHAIN

OUTLINE FILLING

SATIN

(2st.)

LONG & SHORT

(1st.)

FLY VARIATION

(1st.)

BULLION ROSE

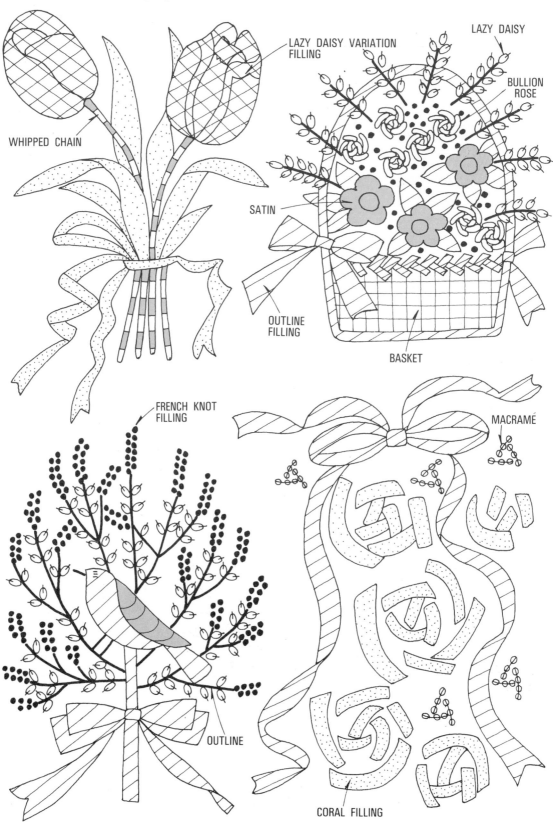

WHIPPED CHAIN

LAZY DAISY VARIATION FILLING

LAZY DAISY

BULLION ROSE

SATIN

OUTLINE FILLING

BASKET

FRENCH KNOT FILLING

MACRAMÉ

OUTLINE

CORAL FILLING

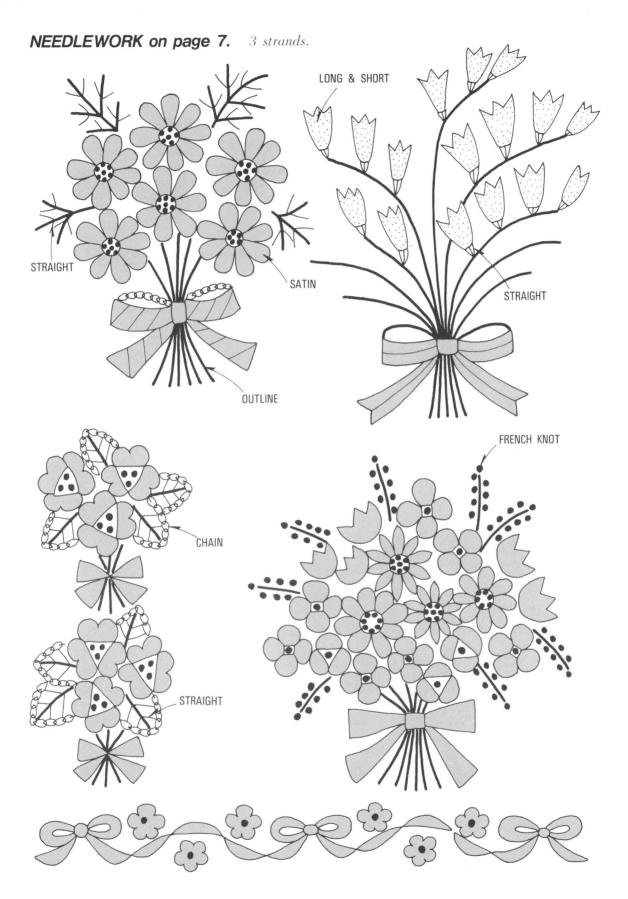

NEEDLEWORK on page 7. *3 strands.*

LONG & SHORT

STRAIGHT

SATIN

STRAIGHT

OUTLINE

CHAIN

FRENCH KNOT

STRAIGHT

NEEDLEWORK on page 8. *With 3 strands except 2 strands for long & short.*

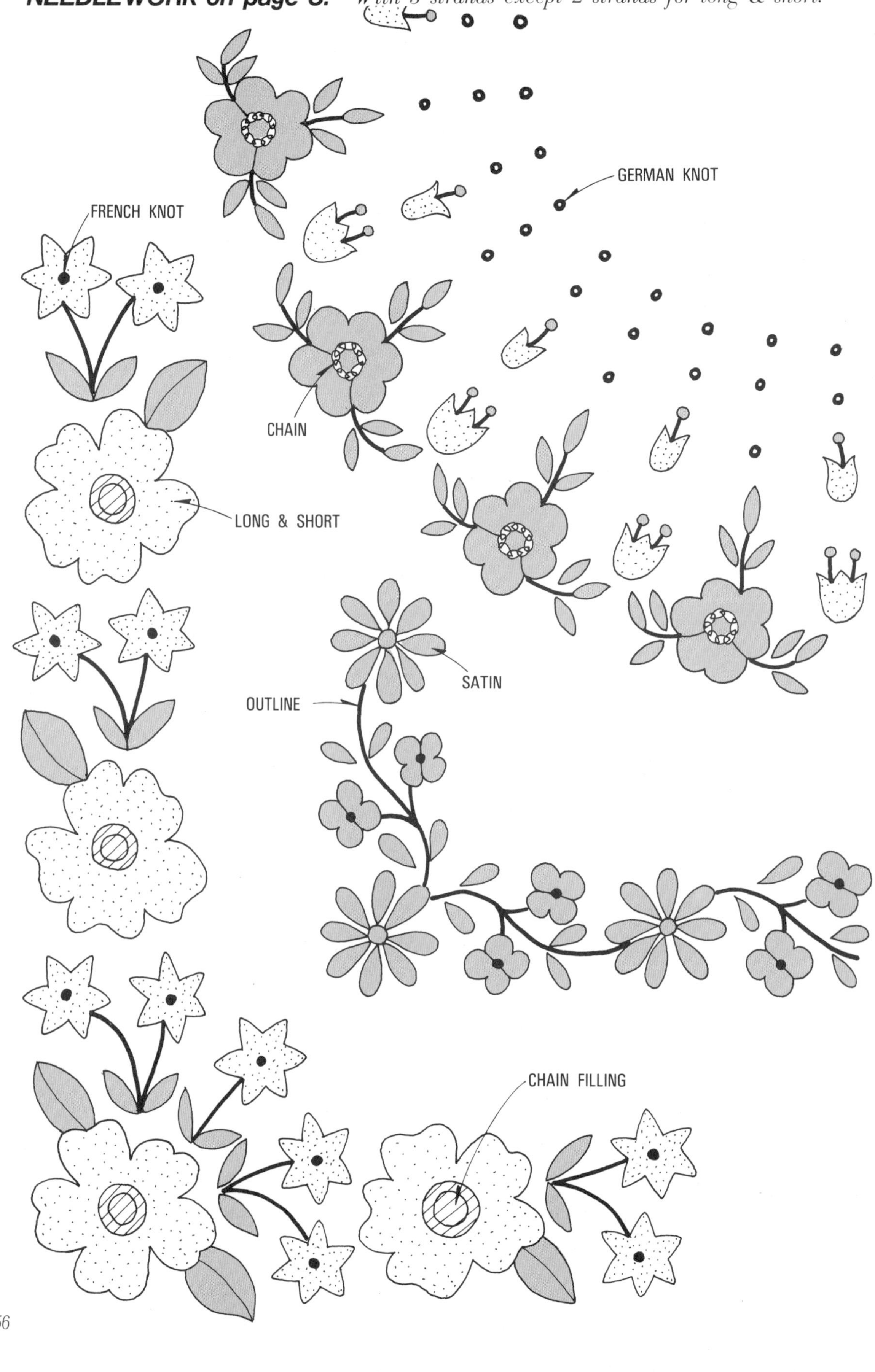

GERMAN KNOT

FRENCH KNOT

CHAIN

LONG & SHORT

OUTLINE

SATIN

CHAIN FILLING

NEEDLEWORK on page 9. *With 3 strands except 2 strands for long & short.*

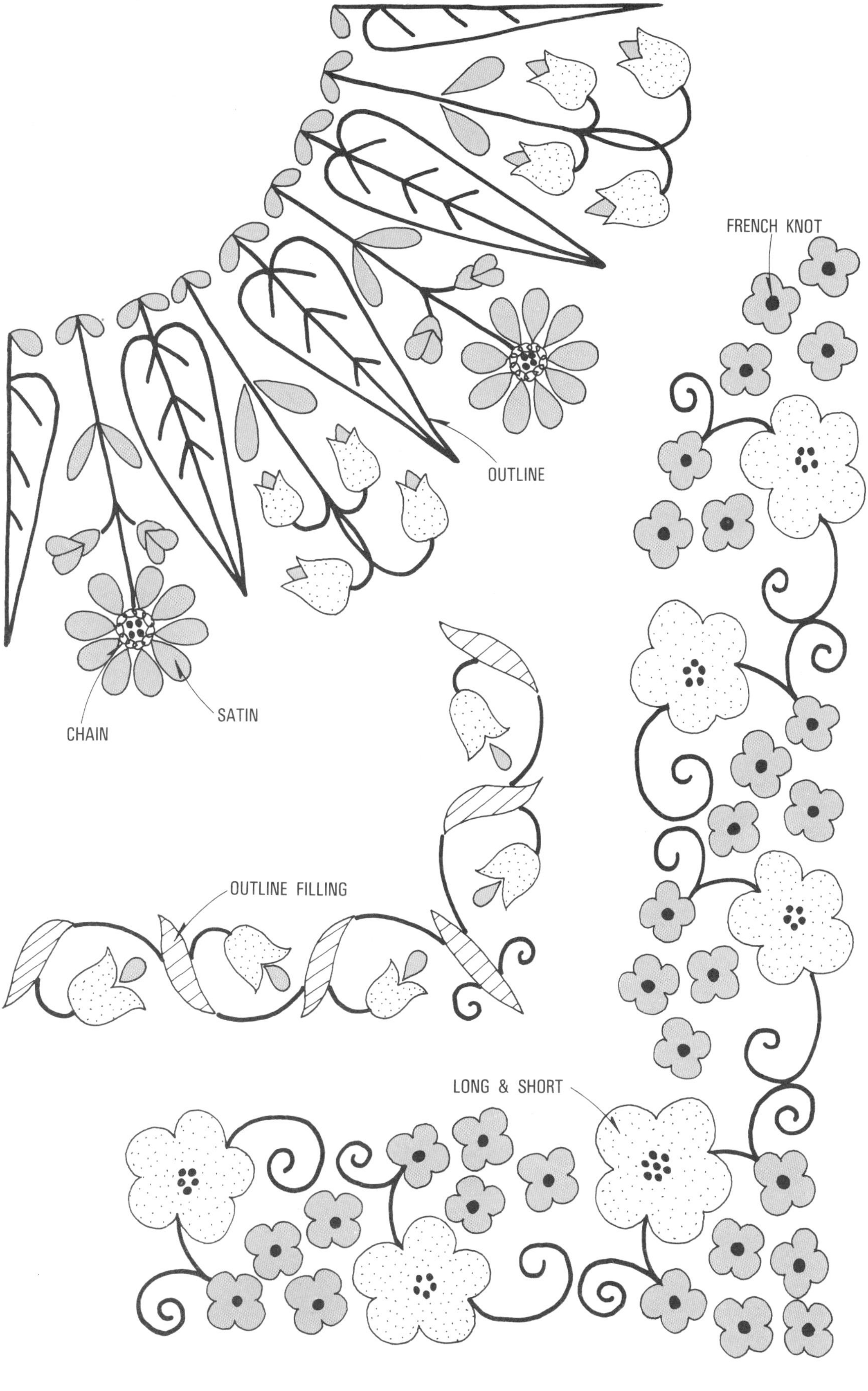

FRENCH KNOT
OUTLINE
SATIN
CHAIN
OUTLINE FILLING
LONG & SHORT

NEEDLEWORK on page 10. *3 strands and satin stitches, unless otherwise specified.*

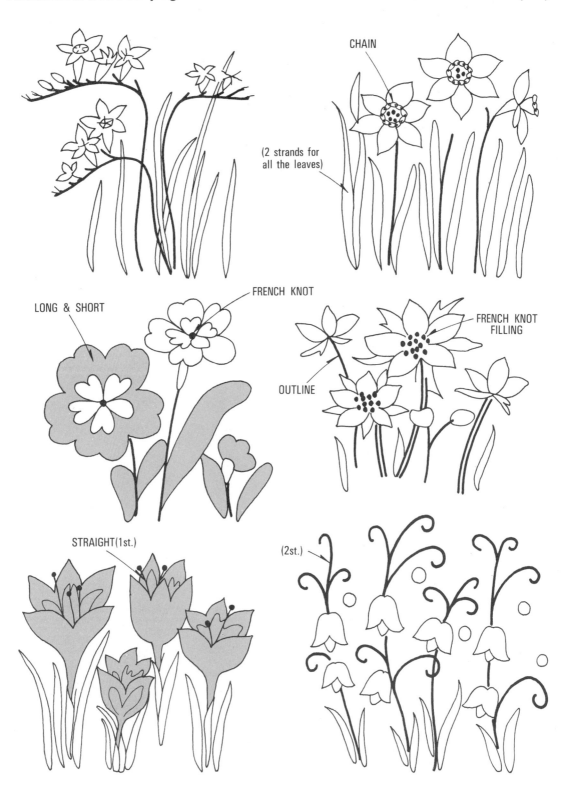

CHAIN

(2 strands for all the leaves)

LONG & SHORT

FRENCH KNOT

FRENCH KNOT FILLING

OUTLINE

STRAIGHT(1st.)

(2st.)

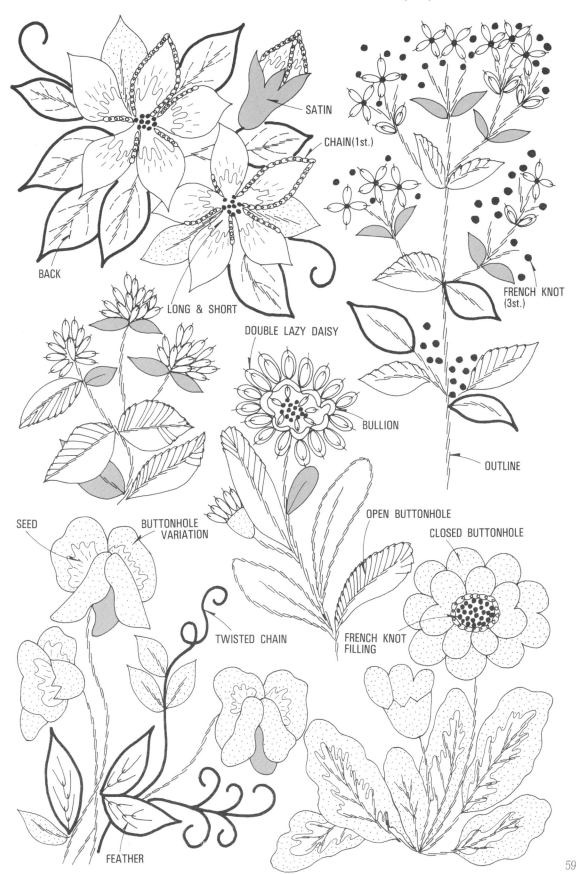

SATIN

CHAIN(1st.)

BACK

FRENCH KNOT
(3st.)

LONG & SHORT

DOUBLE LAZY DAISY

BULLION

OUTLINE

SEED

BUTTONHOLE
VARIATION

OPEN BUTTONHOLE

CLOSED BUTTONHOLE

TWISTED CHAIN

FRENCH KNOT
FILLING

FEATHER

NEEDLEWORK on page 12. *3 strands, unless otherwise specified.*

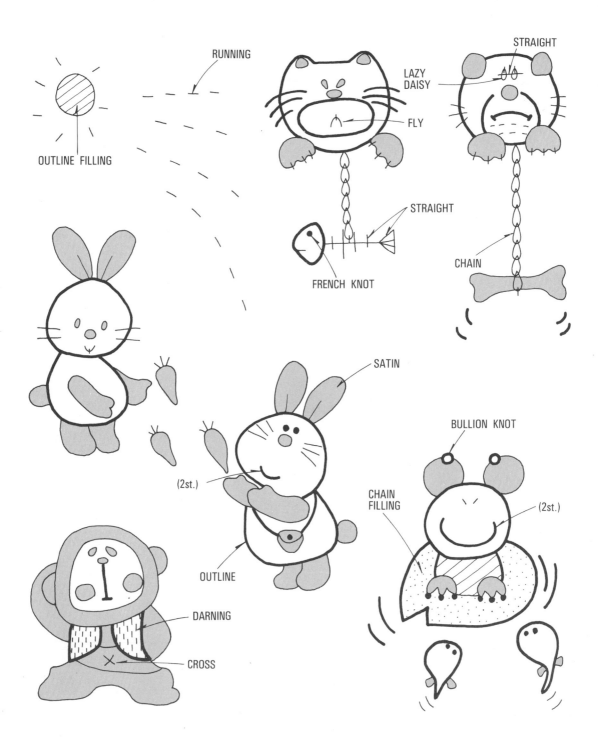

RUNNING

OUTLINE FILLING

LAZY DAISY

STRAIGHT

FLY

STRAIGHT

FRENCH KNOT

CHAIN

SATIN

(2st.)

OUTLINE

BULLION KNOT

CHAIN FILLING

(2st.)

DARNING

CROSS

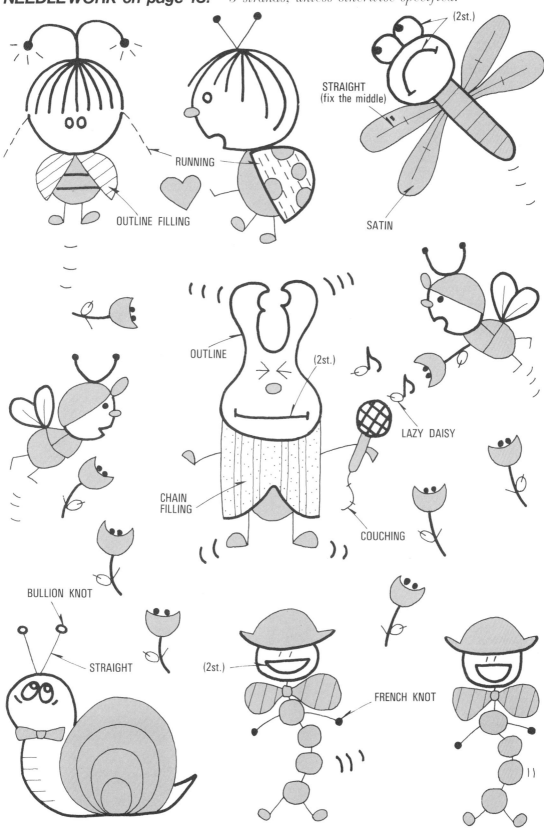

(2st.)

STRAIGHT
(fix the middle)

RUNNING

OUTLINE FILLING

SATIN

OUTLINE

(2st.)

LAZY DAISY

CHAIN
FILLING

COUCHING

BULLION KNOT

STRAIGHT

(2st.)

FRENCH KNOT

NEEDLEWORK on page 14. *3 strands, unless otherwise specified.*

BACK

(2st.)

CHAIN

SATIN

OUTLINE

BULLION KNOT

LAZY DAISY

Secure felt with beads.

CHAIN FILLING

STRAIGHT

NEEDLEWORK on page 15.

3 strands, unless otherwise specified.

(2st.)

Sew beads on.

OUTLINE

CHAIN

STRAIGHT

SATIN

BACK

Secure spangle with beads.

(2st.)

STRAIGHT
OVERCAST

NEEDLEWORK on page 16. *3 strands. unless otherwise specified.*

SLIP(2st.)

FELT

sweet house

OUTLINE

STLAIGHT

営業中

BULLION

BACK(2st.)

OUTLINE FILLING

SATIN

BACK

CHAIN

FRENCH KNOT

OPEN BUTTONHOLE

Sew beads on.

OUTLINE FILLING

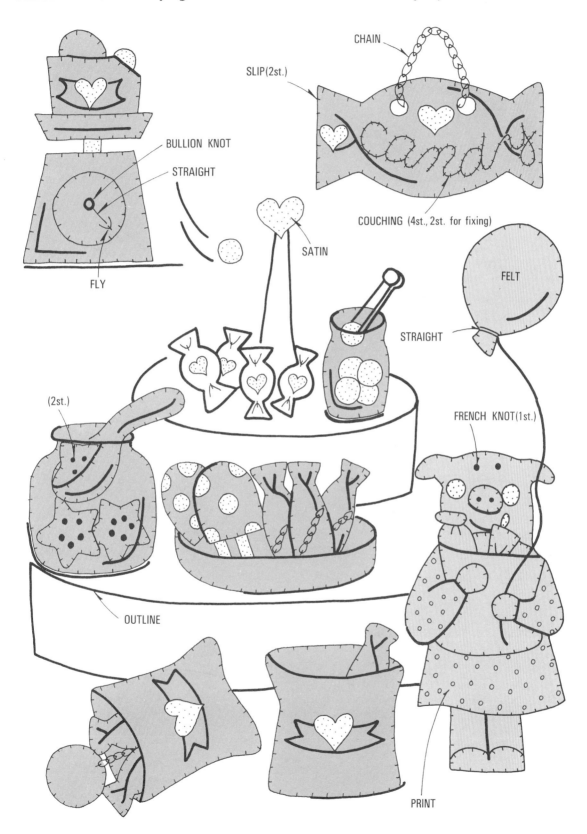

CHAIN

SLIP(2st.)

BULLION KNOT

STRAIGHT

COUCHING (4st., 2st. for fixing)

SATIN

FLY

FELT

STRAIGHT

(2st.)

FRENCH KNOT(1st.)

OUTLINE

PRINT

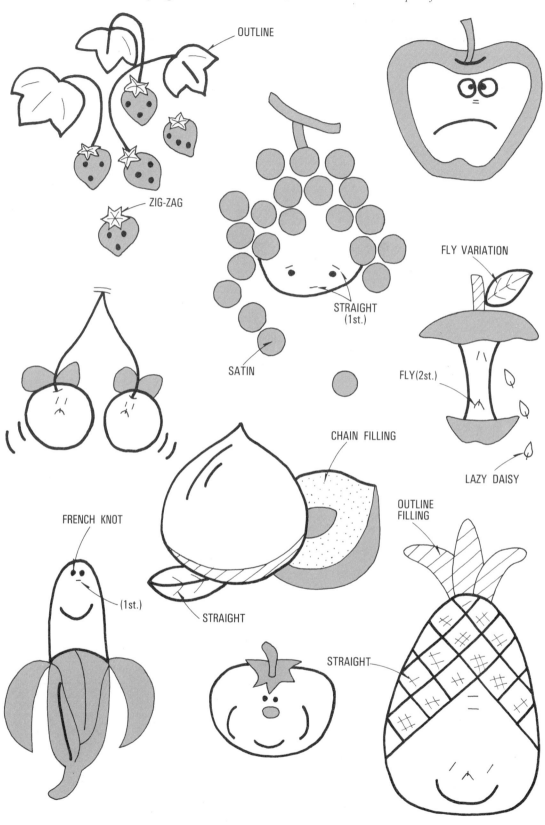

OUTLINE

ZIG-ZAG

STRAIGHT
(1st.)

SATIN

FLY VARIATION

FLY(2st.)

LAZY DAISY

CHAIN FILLING

OUTLINE
FILLING

FRENCH KNOT

(1st.)

STRAIGHT

STRAIGHT

3 strands, unless otherwise specified.

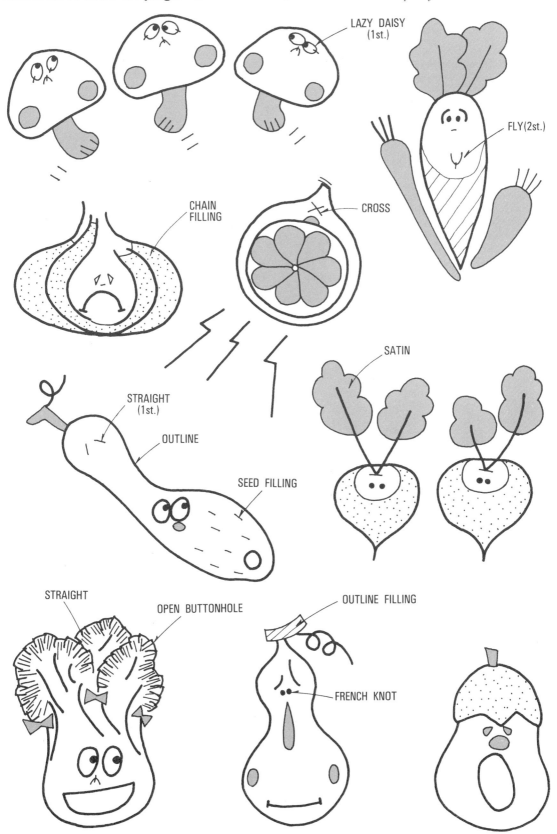

LAZY DAISY (1st.)

FLY (2st.)

CHAIN FILLING

CROSS

SATIN

STRAIGHT (1st.)

OUTLINE

SEED FILLING

STRAIGHT

OPEN BUTTONHOLE

OUTLINE FILLING

FRENCH KNOT

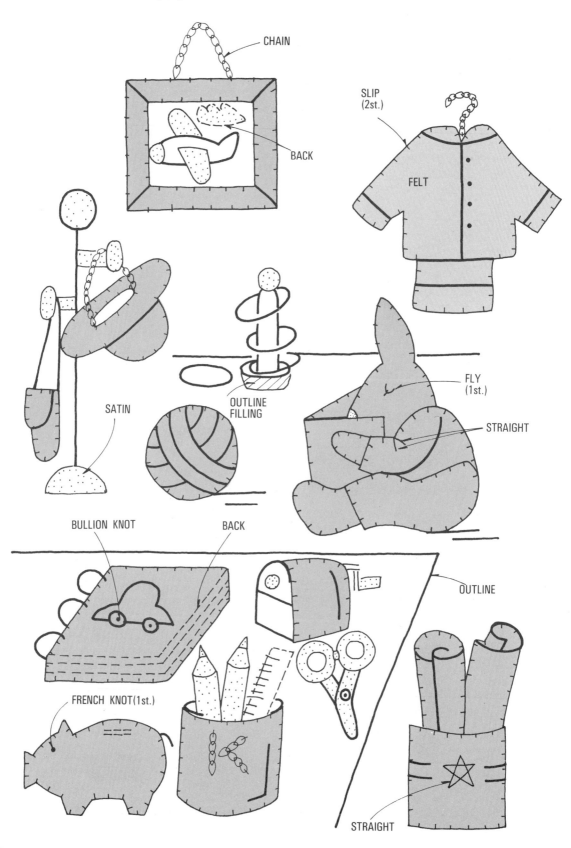

CHAIN

BACK

SLIP
(2st.)

FELT

SATIN

OUTLINE
FILLING

FLY
(1st.)

STRAIGHT

BULLION KNOT

BACK

OUTLINE

FRENCH KNOT(1st.)

STRAIGHT

STRAIGHT

BULLION KNOT

Wind thread on
BULLION KNOT.

SLIP
(2st.)

FELT

OUTLINE FILLING

SATIN

OUTLINE

(2st.)

BACK

NEEDLEWORK on page 22. *3 strands, unless otherwise specified.*

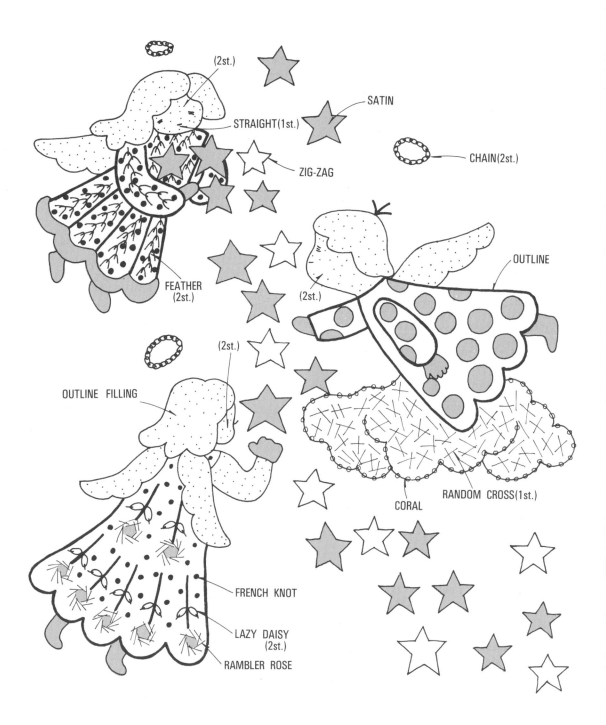

3 strands, unless otherwise specified.

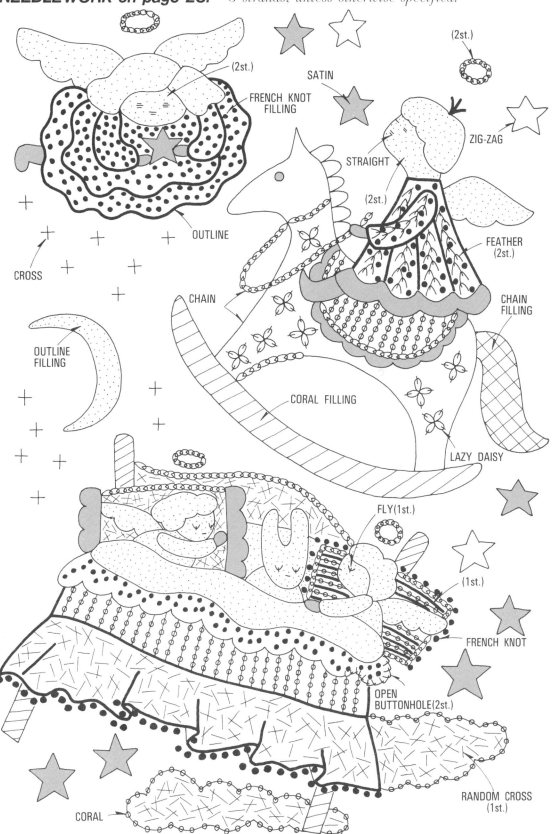

(2st.)

FRENCH KNOT
FILLING

SATIN

(2st.)

ZIG-ZAG

STRAIGHT

(2st.)

FEATHER
(2st.)

OUTLINE

CROSS

CHAIN

CHAIN
FILLING

OUTLINE
FILLING

CORAL FILLING

LAZY DAISY

FLY(1st.)

(1st.)

FRENCH KNOT

OPEN
BUTTONHOLE(2st.)

CORAL

RANDOM CROSS
(1st.)

71

NEEDLEWORK on page 24. *4 strands, unless otherwise specified.*

FRENCH KNOT FILLING

GERMAN KNOT FILLING

CHAIN

CORAL FILLING

TWISTED CHAIN FILLNG

LAZY DAISY

(2st.)

SATIN

OUTLINE

OPEN BUTTONHOLE

FLY

FRENCH KNOT

STRAIGHT

STRAIGHT

LONG & SHORT (3st.)

OUTLINE FILLING

CHAIN FILLING

BUTTONHOLE FILLING

CHAIN

4 strands, unless otherwise specified.

OUTLINE

COOCHED TRELLIS
(3st.)

LONG & SHORT
(3st.)

(3st.)

FRENCH KNOT
FILLING

SURFACE
DARNING

BUTTONHOLE
FILLING

SATIN
(3st.)

BACK

OPEN
BUTTONHOLE

FRENCH KNOT

STRAIGHT
(3st.)

GERMAN
KNOT
FILLING

CORAL
FILLING

CHAIN

OUTLINE
FILLING

FLY

DOUBLE
LAZY DAISY

TWISTED CHAIN

LAZY DAISY

73

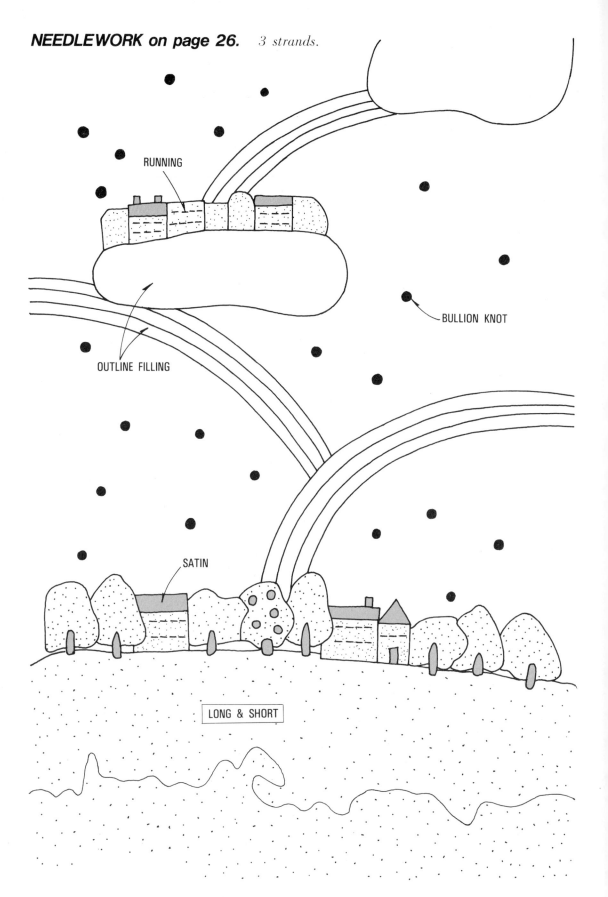

NEEDLEWORK on page 26. *3 strands.*

RUNNING

BULLION KNOT

OUTLINE FILLING

SATIN

LONG & SHORT

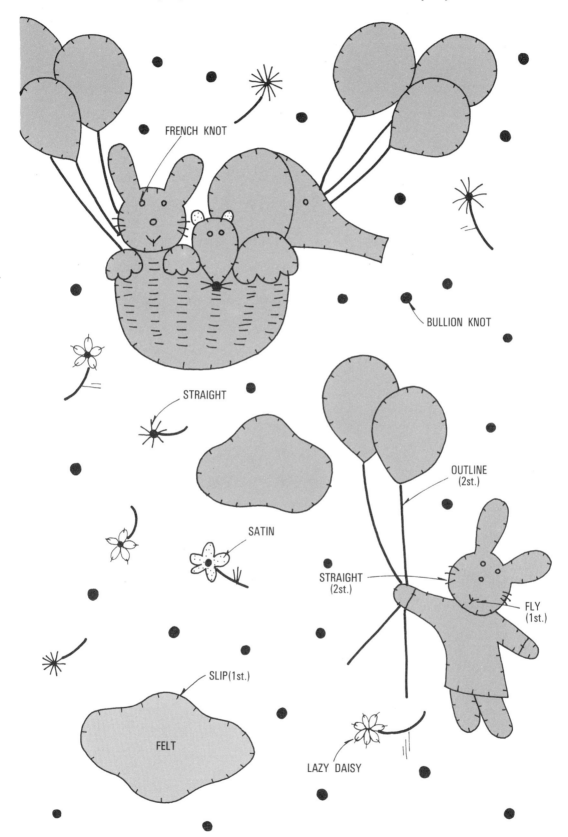

FRENCH KNOT

BULLION KNOT

STRAIGHT

OUTLINE (2st.)

SATIN

STRAIGHT (2st.)

FLY (1st.)

SLIP(1st.)

FELT

LAZY DAISY

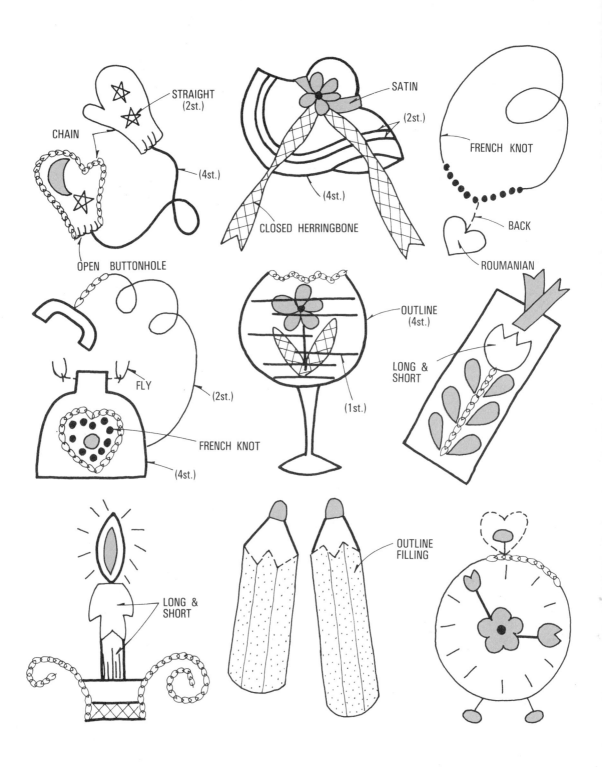

STRAIGHT
(2st.)

CHAIN

(4st.)

OPEN BUTTONHOLE

SATIN

(2st.)

(4st.)

CLOSED HERRINGBONE

FRENCH KNOT

BACK

ROUMANIAN

FLY

(2st.)

FRENCH KNOT

(4st.)

OUTLINE
(4st.)

(1st.)

LONG &
SHORT

LONG &
SHORT

OUTLINE
FILLING

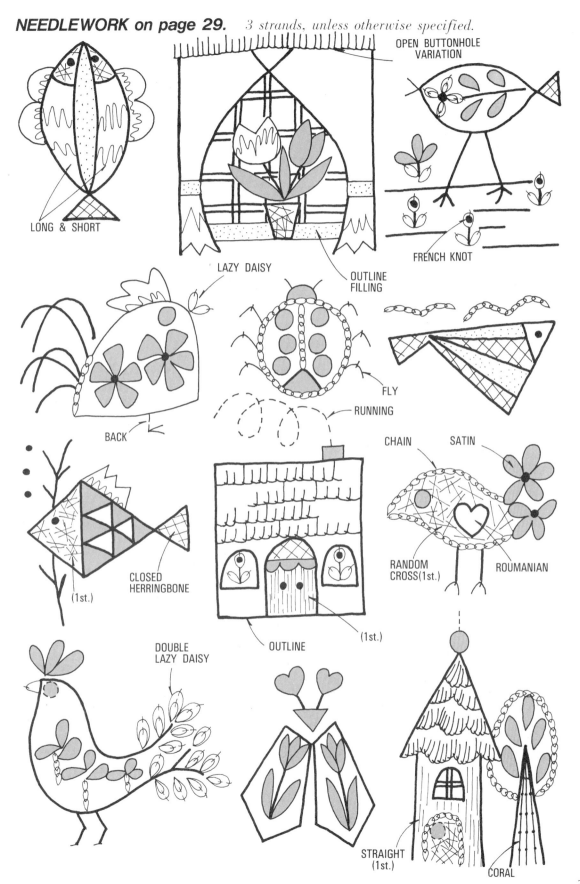

NEEDLEWORK on page 29. *3 strands, unless otherwise specified.*

OPEN BUTTONHOLE VARIATION

LONG & SHORT

LAZY DAISY

OUTLINE FILLING

FRENCH KNOT

BACK

FLY

RUNNING

CHAIN

SATIN

CLOSED HERRINGBONE

(1st.)

RANDOM CROSS (1st.)

ROUMANIAN

DOUBLE LAZY DAISY

OUTLINE

(1st.)

STRAIGHT (1st.)

CORAL

NEEDLEWORK on page 30. *3 strands, unless otherwise specified.*

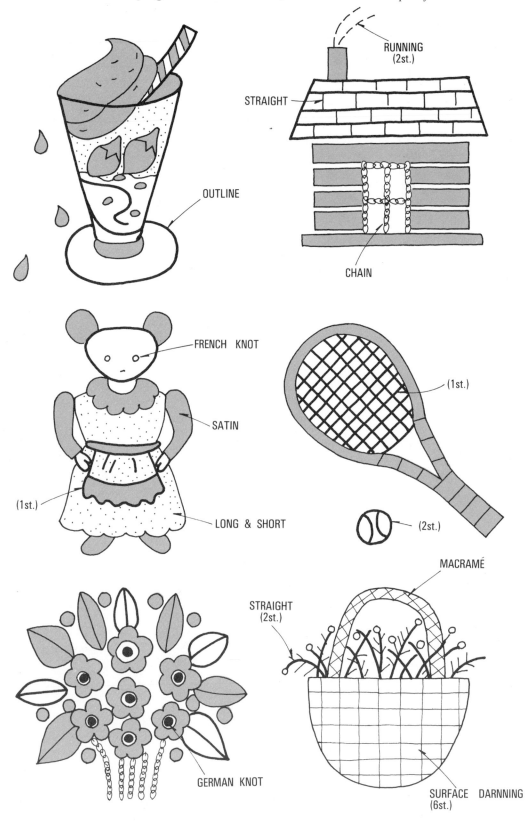

RUNNING
(2st.)

STRAIGHT

CHAIN

OUTLINE

FRENCH KNOT

SATIN

(1st.)

LONG & SHORT

(1st.)

(2st.)

MACRAMÉ

STRAIGHT
(2st.)

GERMAN KNOT

SURFACE DARNNING
(6st.)

NEEDLEWORK on page 31.

3 strands, unless otherwise specified.

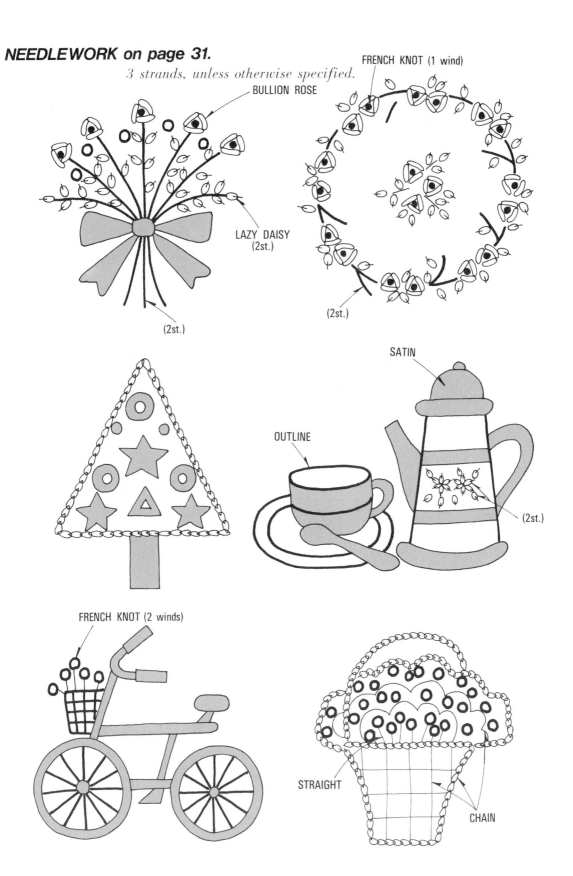

FRENCH KNOT (1 wind)

BULLION ROSE

LAZY DAISY (2st.)

(2st.)

(2st.)

(2st.)

SATIN

OUTLINE

(2st.)

FRENCH KNOT (2 winds)

STRAIGHT

CHAIN

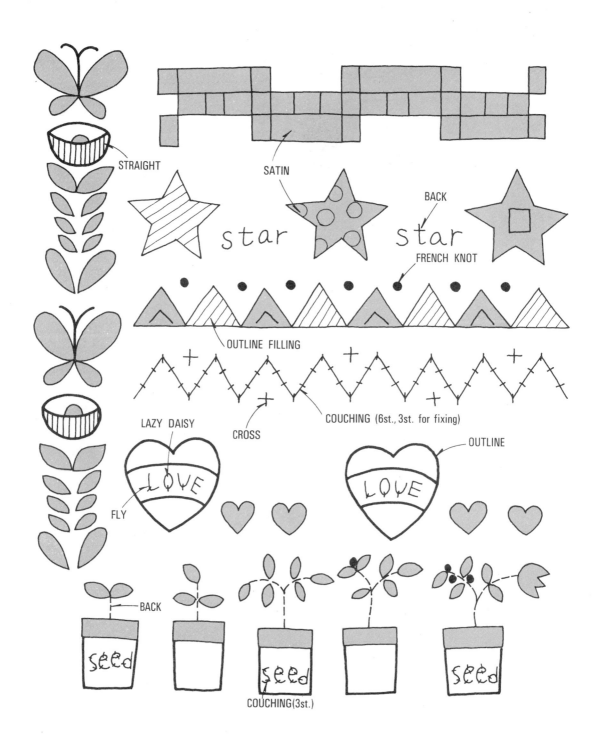

STRAIGHT

SATIN

BACK

star

star

FRENCH KNOT

OUTLINE FILLING

LAZY DAISY

CROSS

COUCHING (6st., 3st. for fixing)

OUTLINE

LOVE

LOVE

FLY

BACK

seed

seed

seed

COUCHING(3st.)

80

mush room

STRAIGHT

carrot ... carrot

SATIN

OUTLINE

Peas

radish   radish

BACK

OUTLINE

glass

FRENCH KNOT

ribbon

SATIN

CUP

BACK

OUTLINE FILLING

box

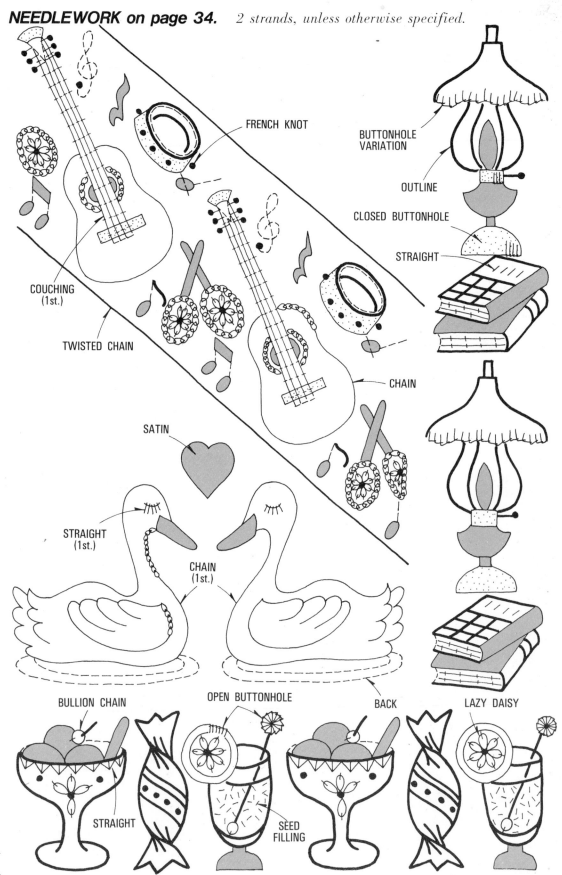

NEEDLEWORK on page 34. *2 strands, unless otherwise specified.*

FRENCH KNOT

BUTTONHOLE VARIATION

OUTLINE

CLOSED BUTTONHOLE

STRAIGHT

COUCHING (1st.)

TWISTED CHAIN

CHAIN

SATIN

STRAIGHT (1st.)

CHAIN (1st.)

BULLION CHAIN

OPEN BUTTONHOLE

BACK

LAZY DAISY

STRAIGHT

SEED FILLING

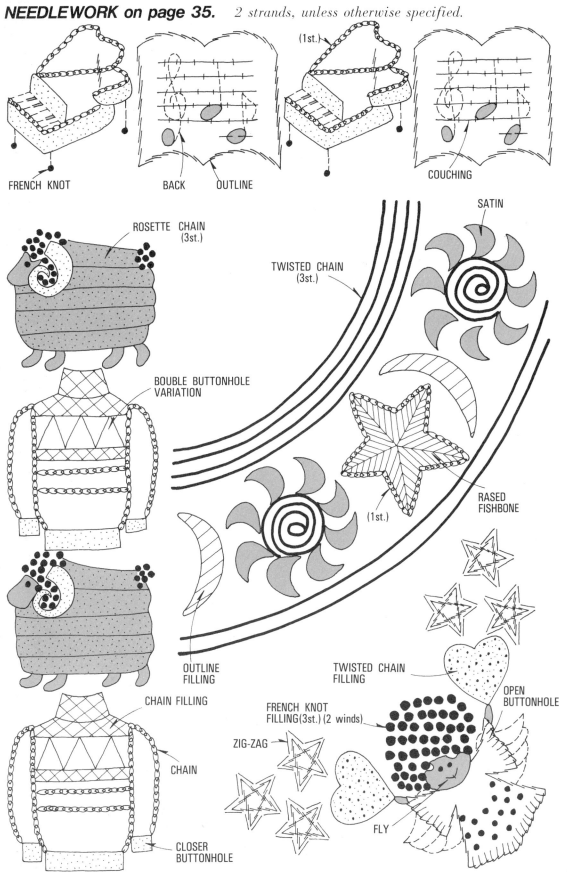

FRENCH KNOT

BACK   OUTLINE

(1st.)

COUCHING

ROSETTE CHAIN
(3st.)

TWISTED CHAIN
(3st.)

SATIN

BOUBLE BUTTONHOLE
VARIATION

RASED
FISHBONE

(1st.)

OUTLINE
FILLING

TWISTED CHAIN
FILLING

CHAIN FILLING

OPEN
BUTTONHOLE

FRENCH KNOT
FILLING(3st.) (2 winds)

CHAIN

ZIG-ZAG

FLY

CLOSER
BUTTONHOLE

NEEDLEWORK on page 36. *2 strands.*

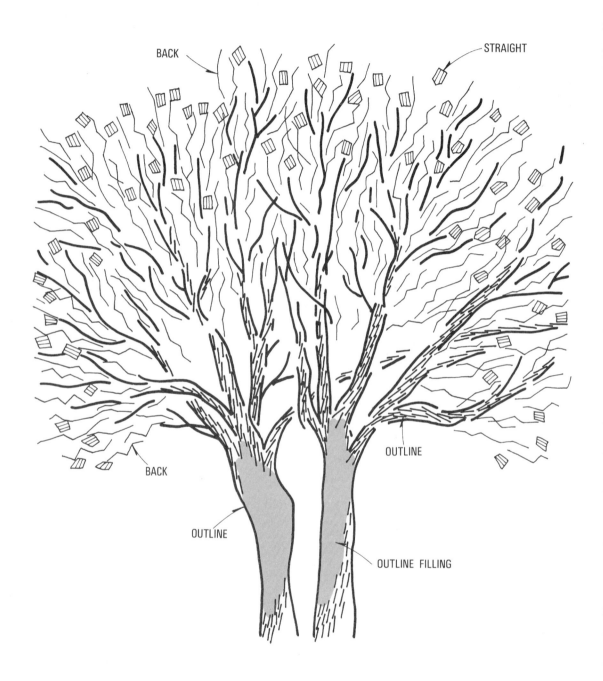

NEEDLEWORK *on page 37.* *2 strands.*

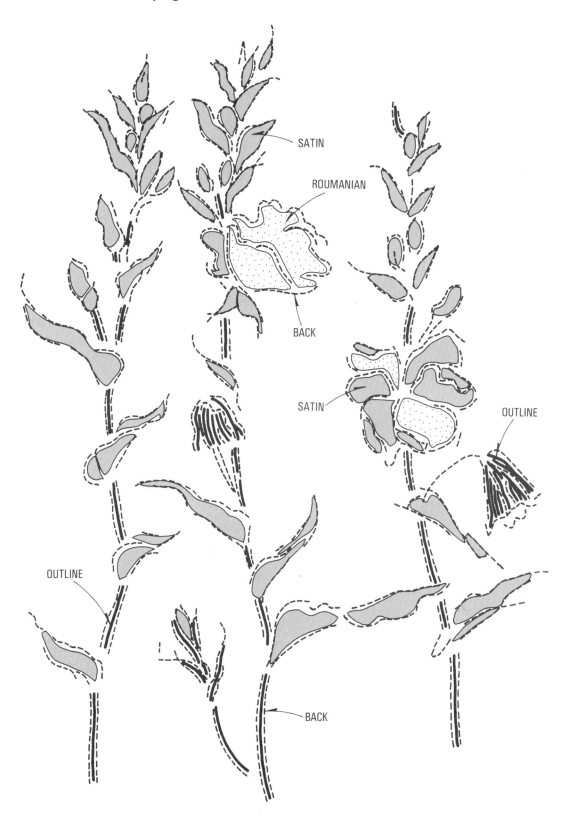

SATIN

ROUMANIAN

BACK

SATIN

OUTLINE

OUTLINE

BACK

NEEDLEWORK on page 38. 2 strands.

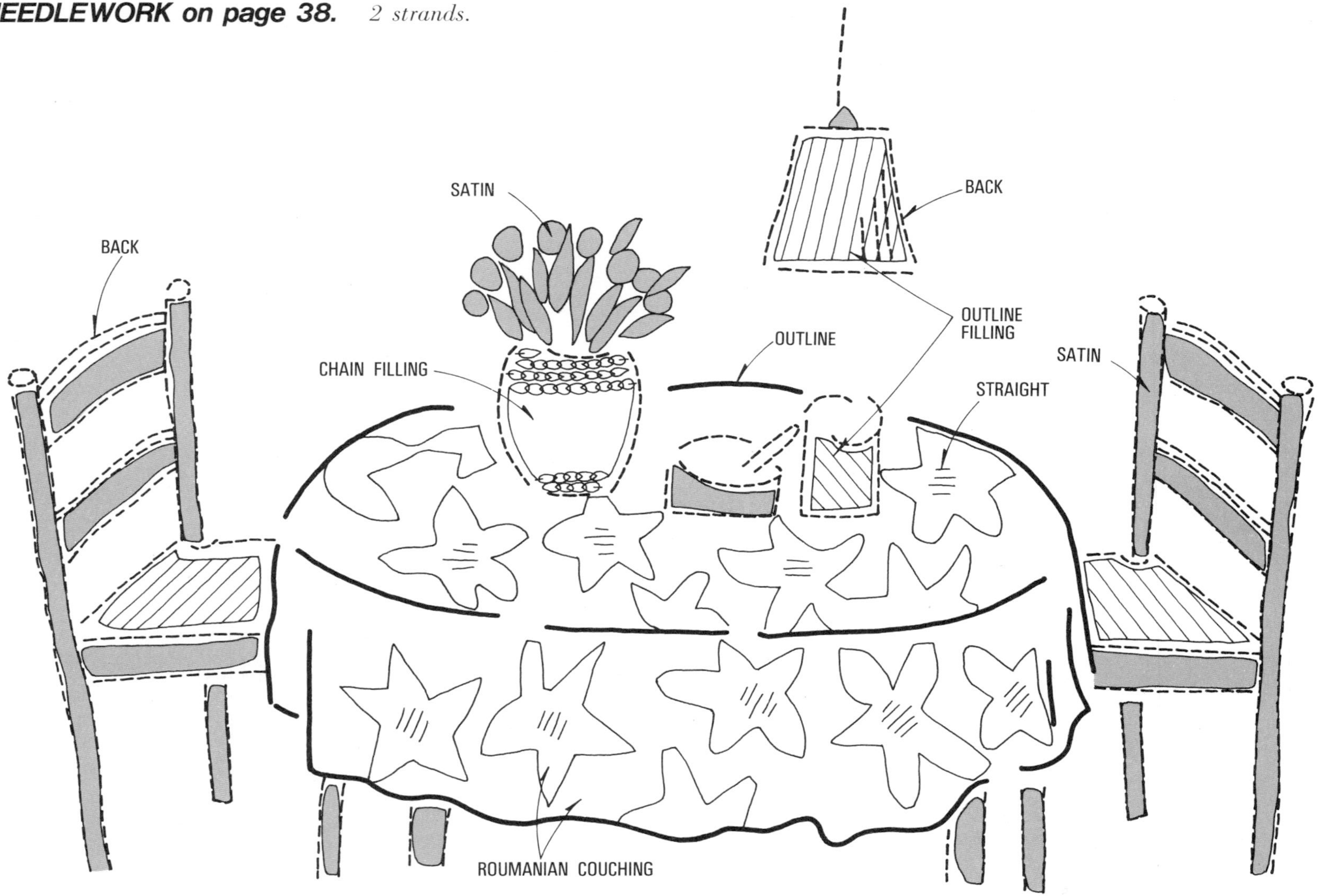

SATIN

BACK

OUTLINE
FILLING

STRAIGHT

OUTLINE

SATIN

CHAIN FILLING

ROUMANIAN COUCHING

BACK

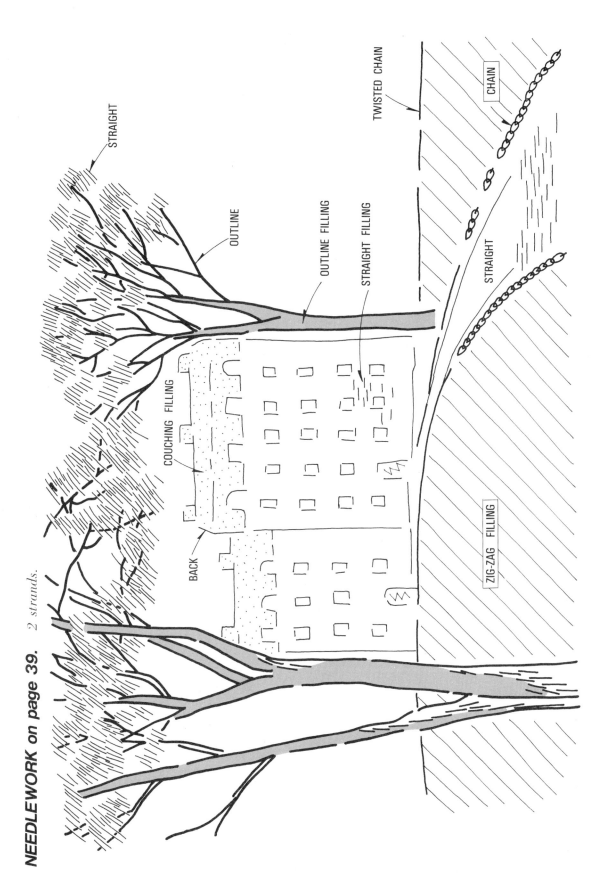

NEEDLEWORK on page **39.** *2 strands.*

STRAIGHT

OUTLINE

OUTLINE FILLING

STRAIGHT FILLING

COUCHING FILLING

BACK

ZIG-ZAG FILLING

STRAIGHT

TWISTED CHAIN

CHAIN

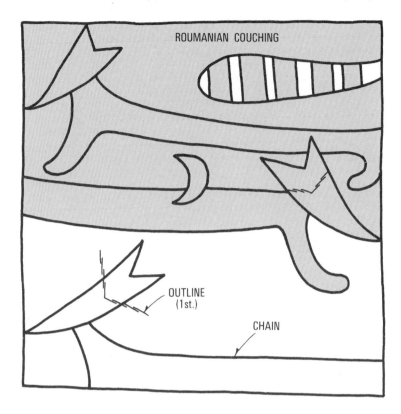

ROUMANIAN COUCHING

OUTLINE
(1st.)

CHAIN

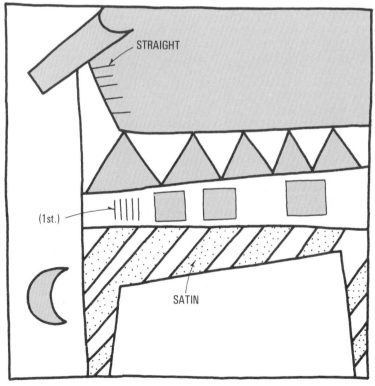

STRAIGHT

(1st.)

SATIN

NEEDLEWORK on page 41. *3 strands, unless otherwise specified.*

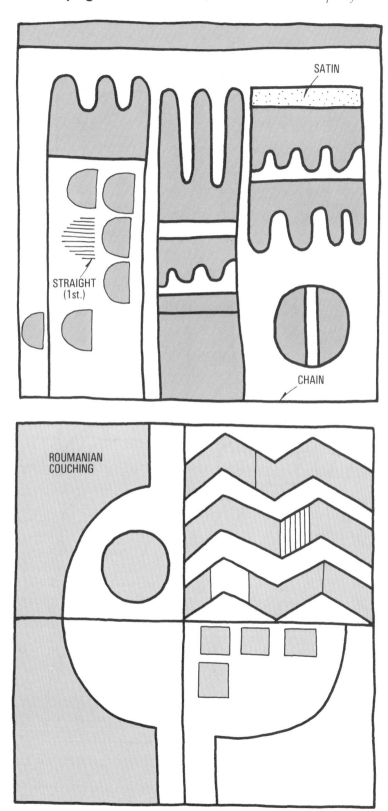

SATIN

STRAIGHT
(1st.)

CHAIN

ROUMANIAN
COUCHING

OUTLINE

CLOSED
BUTTONHOLE

LONG & SHORT

SATIN

OUTLINE

BUTTONHOLE

CHAIN

SATIN

NEEDLEWORK on page 44. *3 strands, unless otherwise specified.*

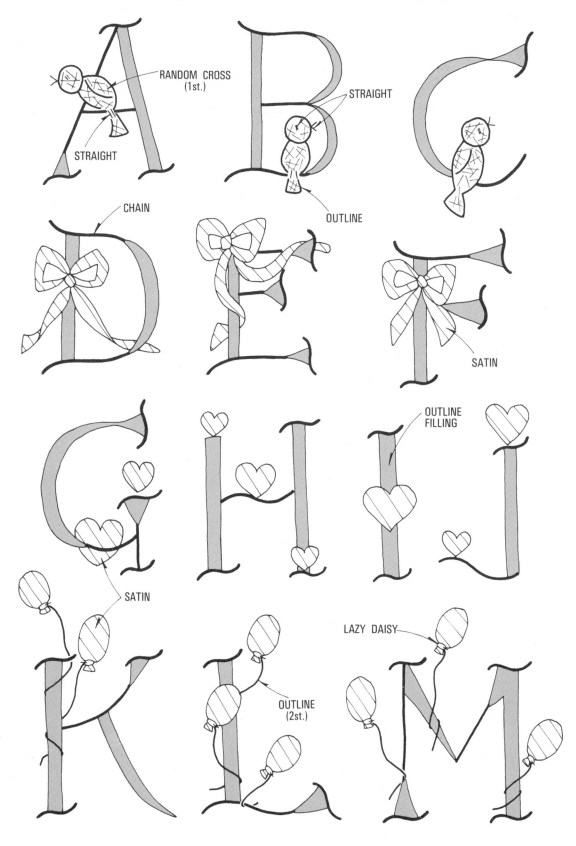

RANDOM CROSS (1st.)

STRAIGHT

STRAIGHT

OUTLINE

CHAIN

SATIN

OUTLINE FILLING

SATIN

LAZY DAISY

OUTLINE (2st.)

NEEDLEWORK on page 45. *3 strands, unless otherwise specified.*

OUTLINE
STRAIGHT
RANDOM CROSS(1st.)
CHAIN
SATIN
OUTLINE EILLING
SATIN
LAZY DAISY
OUTLINE (2st.)

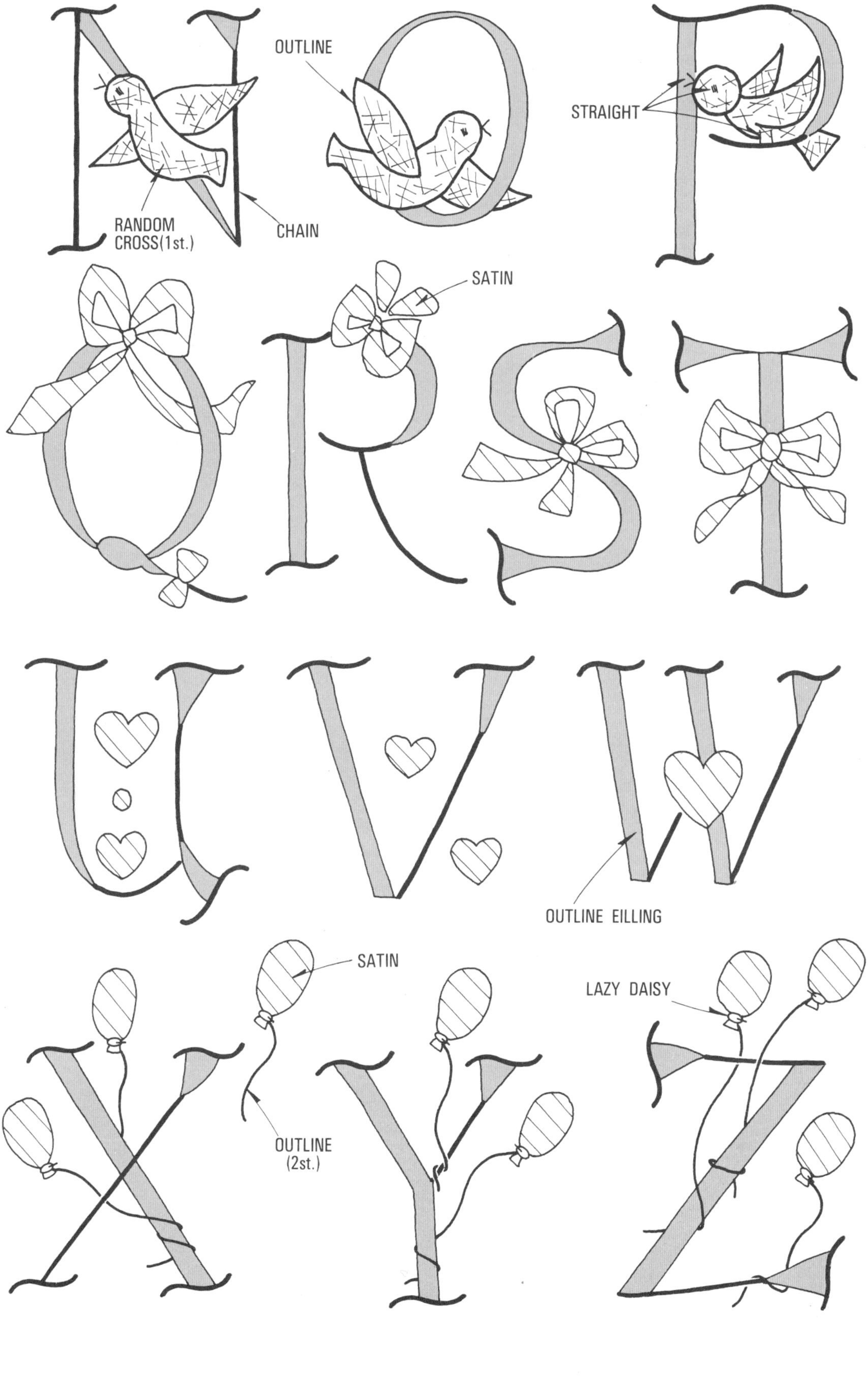

NEEDLEWORK on page 46. *3 strands, unless otherwise specified.*

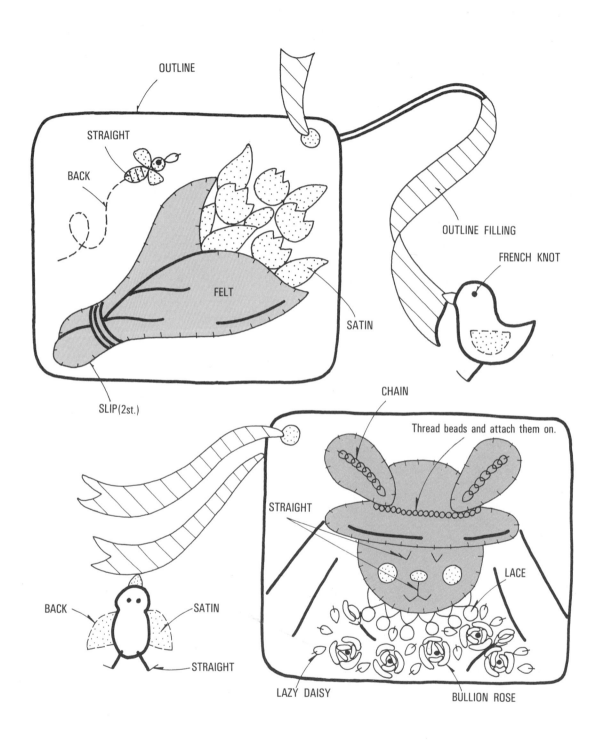

OUTLINE

STRAIGHT

BACK

FELT

SATIN

SLIP(2st.)

OUTLINE FILLING

FRENCH KNOT

CHAIN

Thread beads and attach them on.

STRAIGHT

LACE

BACK

SATIN

STRAIGHT

LAZY DAISY

BULLION ROSE

OUTLINE

FRENCH KNOT

To papa

COUCHING
(6st., 3st. for fixing)

FELT

SLIP(2st.)

BACK

SATIN

OUTLINE FILLING

FLY

To baby

Tie the threads.

STRAIGHT

To mama

Sew beads on.

NEEDLEWORK on page 48. *3 strands, unless otherwise specified.*

FRENCH KNOT
OUTLINE
STRAIGHT
GERMAN KNOT
STRAIGHT
WHIPPED CHAIN

BULLION ROSE (2st.)
OUTLINE FILLING
CORAL(2st.) FILLING
WHIPPED CHAIN(2st.)

SATIN
(2st.)
(2st.)
OUTLINE FILLING

STRAIGHT (2st.)
FRENCH KNOT (2st.)
RUNNING (1st.)
LAZY DAISY

BASIC STITCHES

RUNNING STITCH	DARNING STITCH	BACK STITCH
4 3 2 1		

SEED STITCH	SEED FILLING STITCH	ZIG-ZAG STITCH
3 4 1 2		

OUTLINE STITCH	OUTLINE FILLING STITCH	STRAIGHT OVERCAST

STRAIGHT STITCH	RANDAM CROSS STITCH
1 3 / 1 3 / 2 4 / 2 4 5	

COUCHING	COUCHED TRELLIS STITCH

CHAIN STITCH

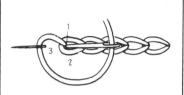

CHAIN FILLING STITCH

WHIPPED CHAIN STITCH

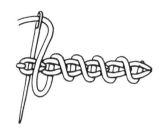

TWISTED CHAIN STITCH

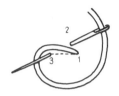
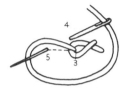

TWISTED CHAIN FILLING STITCH

LAZY DAISY STITCH

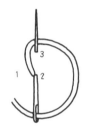

LAZY DAISY VARIATION

DOUBLE LAZY DAISY STITCH

FRENCH KNOT

FRENCH KNOT FILLING

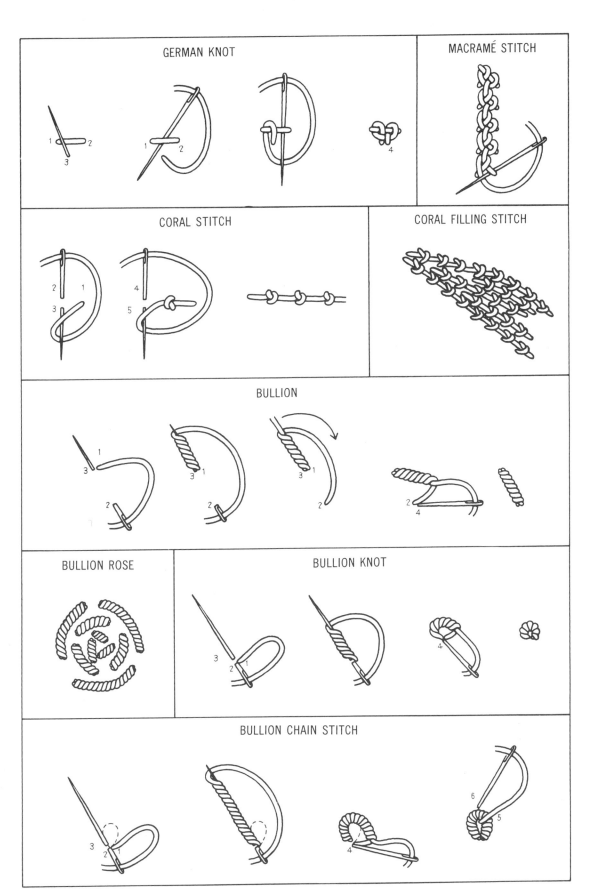

GERMAN KNOT

MACRAMÉ STITCH

CORAL STITCH

CORAL FILLING STITCH

BULLION

BULLION ROSE

BULLION KNOT

BULLION CHAIN STITCH

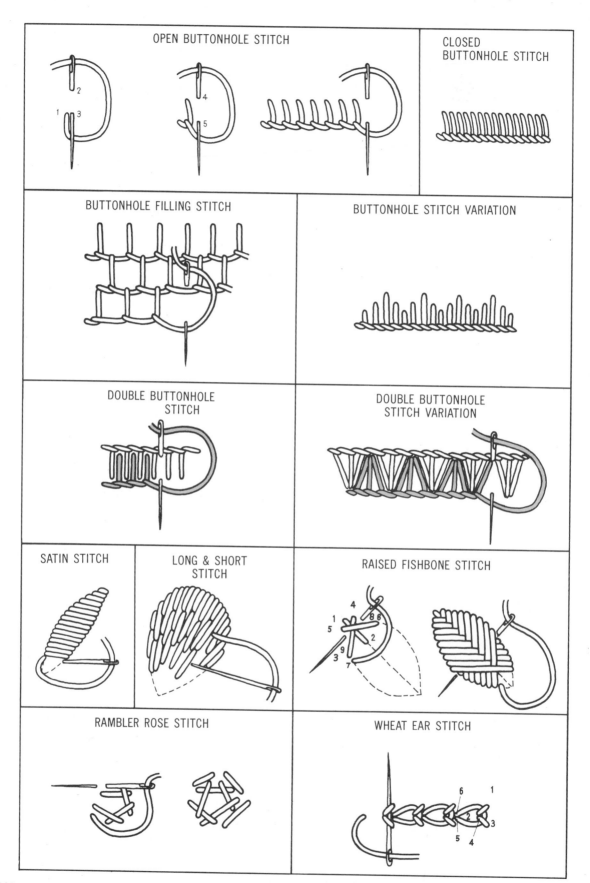

OPEN BUTTONHOLE STITCH

CLOSED BUTTONHOLE STITCH

BUTTONHOLE FILLING STITCH

BUTTONHOLE STITCH VARIATION

DOUBLE BUTTONHOLE STITCH

DOUBLE BUTTONHOLE STITCH VARIATION

SATIN STITCH

LONG & SHORT STITCH

RAISED FISHBONE STITCH

RAMBLER ROSE STITCH

WHEAT EAR STITCH

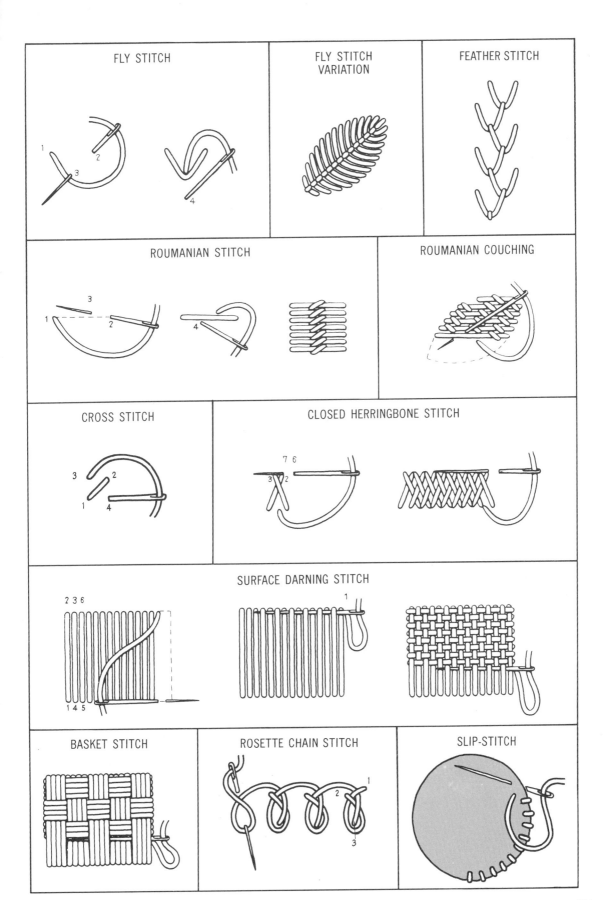

FLY STITCH

FLY STITCH VARIATION

FEATHER STITCH

ROUMANIAN STITCH

ROUMANIAN COUCHING

CROSS STITCH

CLOSED HERRINGBONE STITCH

SURFACE DARNING STITCH

BASKET STITCH

ROSETTE CHAIN STITCH

SLIP-STITCH

EMBROIDERY THREADS

THE MOST POPULAR FOR EMBROIDERY ARE No. 25 and No. 5.

No. 25—One thread consists of 6 strands, and measures 8 m per skein. You can pull out as many threads as required from the bundle if necessary (according to the design).

No. 5—Single thick thread, and is quite lustrous. One skein measures 25 m. Suitable for rough stitches.

Besides these, you have a wide variety of others such as cottons, rayons, silk, wools, even, metal threads. The sizes also range from thick, medium, fine, to extremely fine.

❀ HANDLING THE THREAD

The threads Nos. 25, 5 and 4 come in bundle or ring, depending on the manufacturer. When they are formed in a ring untie the twist, cut one end of the ring with scissors, and pull out one by one. When they are gathered together and held by one or two paper labels, pull out the length from the core of the bundle.

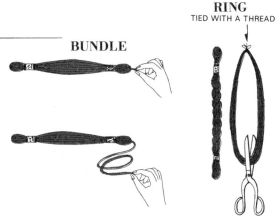

BUNDLE

RING
TIED WITH A THREAD

❀ PASSING THE THREAD THROUGH THE NEEDLE

When you pass 4 strands of the thread through an embroidery needle, fold the ends of the threads, and insert the folded edge through hole of the needle. (See illustration at right). Do the same way when you use a thick yarn like wool.

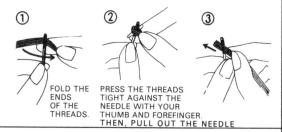

① FOLD THE ENDS OF THE THREADS.

② PRESS THE THREADS TIGHT AGAINST THE NEEDLE WITH YOUR THUMB AND FOREFINGER. THEN, PULL OUT THE NEEDLE

③

HINTS ON STITCHING

❀ HOW TO START AND END STITCHING

A securing knot is rarely made in embroidery. To start stitching, see the illustration below. If you need to make a knot, form a small loop round the needle, and gently pull out the needle, with your left thumb pressing the loop.

GENERAL STITCHING

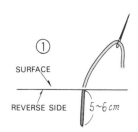

① SURFACE

REVERSE SIDE 5~6 cm

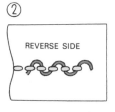

② REVERSE SIDE

SEW THROUGH THE STITCHES ON THE REVERSE SIDE (NOT SHOWING ON THE SURFACE WHEN STARTING OR ENDING THE SEAM).

FILLING STITCHING

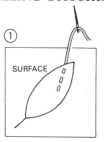

① SURFACE

SEW A FEW STITCHES TOWARD THE STARTING POINT.

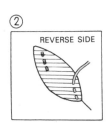

② REVERSE SIDE

SEW BACK A FEW STITCHES BEFORE BREAKING OFF (WITH CARE TO NOT SHOW THE SEAM ON FRONT).

HOW TO TRANSFER A DESIGN

Place a sheet of thin paper over the design, and copy it drawing with a hard (lead) pencil.

✿ USING TRACING PAPER

Place the waxed side of the tracing paper—the kind made for dressmaking—down on the right side of the material pinned to a board. Put the thin paper with design over the tracing paper, and work a round carefully with a steel pen, a hard pencil, or a tracing wheel.

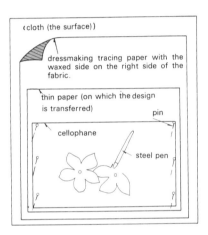

(cloth (the surface))

dressmaking tracing paper with the waxed side on the right side of the fabric.

thin paper (on which the design is transferred)

pin

cellophane

steel pen

✿ USING A GLASS PLATE

Bridge two boxes with a piece of opaque glass (to minimize eyestrain) and put a lighted bulb under the glass. Transfer a design found in book onto thin paper. Then put the paper on the glass, lay the material on it and outline directly on the material with a hard pencil.

✿ USING TISSUE PAPER

Trace the design onto a sheet of smooth tissue paper, and tack this into position at the edge of the background material. Using a basting thread, tack around the whole of the design through the tissue paper and material. Embroider over it, then remove the paper.

ENLARGING THE DESIGN

Draw a graph with right squares over the design. The more complicated the design, the smaller the squares. Then draw in another piece of paper the squares that are enlarged at regular rate, and trace the design in the enlarged graph. Do the opposite when reducing the design.